Tundra Talk

LESSONS
FROM THE BERRY PATCH

DORIS VAN AMBURG

WESTBOW
PRESS®
A DIVISION OF THOMAS NELSON
& ZONDERVAN

WestBow Press books may be ordered through
booksellers or by contacting:

WestBow Press
A Division of Thomas Nelson & Zondervan
1663 Liberty Drive
Bloomington, IN 47403
www.westbowpress.com
1 (866) 928-1240

ISBN: 978-1-5127-7623-2 (sc)
ISBN: 978-1-5127-7624-9 (e)

Library of Congress Control Number: 2017902580

Print information available on the last page.

WestBow Press rev. date: 02/24/2017

This book is dedicated to my parents, George and Evelyn Heater, who gave this country girl wings to fly all the way to Alaska. Thank you, Mom and Dad!

Introduction

The Alaskan Arctic tundra awaits as I walk out the door with water boots on my feet. Buckets are in my hand. I am heading to God's garden to pick blueberries. My family and I live about seventy-five miles north of the Arctic Circle in the Iñupiat village of Noatak. Just about two hundred yards from my back door lies the entire northern slope of this great state. The landscape is covered with the bounty and richness of many edible plants that have been lovingly placed here by the hand of God. Blueberries are often the fruit of choice, and there is a great abundance of them.

Today the breeze blows in my face, bringing the fresh outdoor smells of tundra. I close my eyes and breathe in deep; my senses are alive, my mind is clear, and I recognize the hand of God in my surroundings.

I have spent many hours on the tundra in this garden. I call it God's garden because it is a garden I neither planted nor watered, yet it has been faithful to produce fruit and to bless our freezer and our family every year—and not just mine alone but anyone who is willing to take the time and effort to gather these berries. Blessings from God.

Hundreds of times I have bent to pluck these small berries, fruit in its season, from the mother plant. And many times God has brought to my mind spiritual thoughts, life truths, convictions, love, and verses that remind me that we are His fruit, that we are commanded to bear fruit, that we are to take on fruit, and that we are to give fruit. Time in the berry patch has brought wisdom and teaching to my heart. There are many applications and admonitions that the word of God touches on concerning the subject of fruit and how I can apply that to my life.

Most of the lessons presented in this devotional aren't specific to just a blueberry patch but could apply to many kinds of fruit. They are, however, truths from God's word and applications for our lives that we might be enriched and in turn enrich others and build up God's church and His kingdom.

The Beginning

"In the beginning God created the heavens and the earth" (Genesis 1:1). And in the beginning when the Arctic was created, God planted the seeds of the blueberry bushes that grow across the spans of the tundra. The beginning. The starting. It all started with a seed that grew into a plant that, in turn, produced a beautiful blossom.

In the beginning our souls are awakened. The seed of God's word is planted and takes root in our hearts, and it begins to grow and blossom and flourish. We accept salvation. We believe and accept the message of God's grace, and we allow forgiveness from Him to flow into our hearts and souls. This grace produces beauty and blesses our lives and relationships. The love of God buds and blooms. People notice. We have become witnesses, living testimonies. It is beautiful and attractive.

The Arctic tundra is a harsh environment. It is

subjected to below-freezing temperatures for about eight months every year. In addition to the cold, the tundra is also void of much sunlight during these months. And to add to these hardships, this area is considered to be an arctic desert because the climate is so dry and the snow that does fall contains so little moisture. Yet every spring I marvel at the beauty that explodes in the sunlight and warmth. Beautiful blooms and blossoms are everywhere!

Out of the harshness of our lives—the sin, turmoil, disappointment, regrets, and unmet expectations— we come to God. And even so, we blossom because of His grace and His love. Because of His forgiveness, we can forgive, let go, and break free. And we bloom!

In our blooming there is hope and expectation. God is at work. He is moving and creating and redeeming. There is change. There is growth. There is life! And God isn't finished with us yet. This is only the beginning—a beautiful beginning of a journey of growing and changing—a journey of becoming.

> For it is by grace you have been saved, through faith and this not from yourselves it is the gift of God—not by works, so that no one can boast. For we are God's workmanship, created in Christ Jesus to do good works, which God prepared in advance for us to do. (Ephesians 2:8–10)

Quiet Growth

The waiting. Forming. Rains come and go. Changing. The winds blow. Growing. The summer sun moves around the sky from north to east, then south to west, until finally it has come full circle—repeating this for many days, never dropping below the horizon. In some ways, monotony has set in. The blossom fades and is replaced by a seemingly worthless small, hard, round ball. Ever so slightly and slowly, in the land that now knows no night, in never-ending light, there is change. The beauty of the blossom is gone. People pass by unnoticing—not even a glance. But there is growth—slow and steady in exposure to the light and rain and wind.

Is this us? Is this my life? Christ becomes alive in us, and there is great joy and excitement. As true as these are, they turn into everyday ups and downs: a celebration, a trial, a birth, a sickness, trouble with children, trouble with parents, a promotion, a new job, an engagement, a loss, coffee with a friend, or support from our Sunday school class. All these roll together to make life. The blossom of the newness has faded.

And all these—the trials and hardships, the joy and the fun—begin to build us in faith, strength, and courage. And we grow. We trust. We put our hope in God's word and in His promises. We read our Bibles and see the examples of the men and women of faith; we realize that the imperfections of humanity reach to us too—to me and you. And we continue to walk, putting one foot in front of the other. And we can't see God.

Then we catch a glimpse of Him—a phone call, an answered prayer, a paycheck, or a hand to hold in the hard times. And we grow. And we grow some more. And we stay attached to the vine and draw from Him. Living and alive in the land of light—spiritual light—the never-ending light of his love. And while people may pass unnoticing, our hearts are growing and changing because of the presence of God.

The blossom has faded, but the fruit is growing. There is change. It may not be beautiful in this stage of life, but it is growing, and it is a product of God's power and love at work in our lives.

> Consider it pure joy, my brothers, whenever you face trials of many kinds, because you know that the testing of your

faith develops perseverance. Perseverance must finish its work so that you may be mature and complete, not lacking anything. (James 1:2–5)

Who Is the Gardener?

Sometimes I don't like the weather conditions—it is too hot or too cold, too rainy, too dry, or too windy. It seems I can be hard to please. Nevertheless, the fruit on the tundra grows, and the God who controls the weather and seasons is in control of our lives—mine and yours— and is creating conditions for fruit to grow in us!

So you're thinking, *Not so fun*. You're right. Our life in Christ isn't about fun. It's about growing, changing, and maturing. We can't do this if there is too much sunshine and beautiful weather. We need some rain sometimes. We can't see the sun when it is raining, yet we have faith the sun is still up there in the sky and will reappear tomorrow (or someday). And it does.

If we hold our thumb out at arm's length and close one eye, we can block out our view of the sun. Something as small as our own thumb can block out the huge sun of our solar system! Sometimes trials and troubles in our lives seem to block out the Son. Do I ever let my circumstances block out my Savior, the Son of my soul?

Summers in the Arctic are short, and I tend to want lots of nice weather so I can enjoy being outside. I love feeling the warmth of the sun on my skin. Much of the year I am forced to stay bundled up and protected from the cold, or I have to stay covered to keep the mosquitoes off my skin. But the rains do come. And sometimes I grumble. I would rather be boating or fishing or camping. Yet thanks to the rain, the berries on the tundra are growing.

Our lives are like that. Trials come—temptations, troubles, and betrayal. We can't see God. We can't feel His presence. The warmth of the sun is gone. But we stay, we pray, and we open God's word and take to heart His promises. We determine to trust and put our faith even in our unseen God. And we grow. Faith arises. The Son shines. Relationships may or may not be restored. Health may or may not come. Finances may or may not change. But God keeps us and strengthens us. He pours grace into our hearts in the midst of our trials and struggles. And when we come through on the other side, we realize He was with us all along. And we grow.

Thank you, Lord. Help me to accept the rain as well as the sunshine, knowing it is all from you and that you are in control. God is the grower of the fruit, both on the tundra and in my life!

Every good and perfect gift is from above, coming down from the Father of the heavenly lights, who does not change like shifting shadows. (James 1:17)

Take Time—God's Time

Blue on the top and green on the bottom. "Not yet," I tell my children who have just scampered in from playing outside, excitement in their voices as they talk over each other in a hurry to tell me the berries are ripe. As much as they do not enjoy picking when we go to the patch, they do enjoy the eating! But if they get in a hurry and rush the process, the result is a hard, sour berry. Not yet.

Do we ever get in a hurry and God says, "Not yet"? Do we rush others whose response is "not yet"? There is a right and proper time for everything. If we rush it, the results can be hard and sour. No good. Not worth the effort. Like a sour berry, we feel like spitting it out.

We live in a culture that tends to want things now. We don't like to wait in line for our already "fast" food. We have microwaves to speed up cooking and choppers to speed up chopping. We have every sort of modern gadget to save us time. But tragedy and calamity can strike when we try to incorporate that mind-set into our spiritual lives.

We can't rush God. Growing and ripening take time. Time. We don't want to wait. We don't have time to wait. Yet that is God's style—His plan. He has a journey planned. The journey is a process. It's not just about the end result; it's about getting there!

In our lives, we are growing fruit. We are growing character, skills, habits, and disciplines that can, should, and will have a positive effect on us, our families, and others around us. God is perfecting this fruit in our lives. We see it growing and developing. But caution: let us not become disheartened during the process. Let us lean in on God. We must trust in Him as He develops and hones our lives, hearts, and characters into what is pleasing and mature. Let us submit to Him and allow Him to complete this process in us, that we may be mature fruit that will be used to further His kingdom.

> I thank my God every time I remember you. In all my prayers for all of you, I always pray with joy because of your partnership in the gospel from the first day until now, being confident of this, that he who began a good work in you will carry it on to completion until the day of Christ Jesus. (Philippians 1:3–6)

Hide and Seek

I stand up to catch the breeze, shoo away a few mosquitos, and wipe the sweat off my forehead. The breeze is refreshing. I bend down again to continue picking. The berries are ripe. But the leaves are full and green, and the berries tend to hide behind the green of the leaves. Picking berries at this stage requires much bending and searching and pushing branches aside so the fruit underneath can be revealed.

Hmmm. What does this scenario have to do with my life? Or yours? Let's explore our hearts for a while. We have been blessed with God-given potential that has blossomed and grown and ripened. But what am I doing with it? Is it hiding? Am I burying my talents? Does my church need a Sunday school teacher or a worship leader. Is someone in need of prayer? Has God placed a call on my life to be a nurse, lawyer, teacher, or missionary?

As believers, we are all called to bear fruit, and God

bestows the gift of this fruit upon us. He plants seeds in our heart, grows them, and causes them to mature. But then we have our part. What will we do with it? When God calls us out or up or on to use these gifts, talents, and fruits, it is for His glory. It is for the building and strengthening of His body. He gives us talents and abilities that bless others around us and builds them up in Christ.

It is easy to be fearful like many of the Bible heroes and heroines we read about—to hide behind our youth, our smallness, our lack of education. Maybe we think we lack experience or training. But when God calls us, He equips us. Over and over in scripture we have examples of men and women who were called to have a part in the kingdom of God, who felt inadequate, but as they stepped out and up and put their faith and confidence in God, God showed up in great ways! The seas parted, the walls came down, the axe head floated, the walls went up, and the giants came down. "Is anything too difficult for God?" (Genesis 18:14).

God is still God! He has blessed us and equipped us. Let us not hide our fruit from Him. Let us be faithful in allowing God to use what He has grown in us for His kingdom and His glory. Amen and amen.

> May the God of peace, who through the
> blood of the eternal covenant brought

back from the dead our Lord Jesus, that great Shepherd of the sheep, equip us with everything good for doing his will and may he work in us what is pleasing to him, through Jesus Christ, to whom be glory for ever and ever. Amen. (Hebrew 13:20–21)

Coming Clean

*M*uffin batter rested in the bowl on the counter waiting for the last ingredient. I opened the Ziploc freezer bag and began to spill the berries in to the measuring cup. Oh dear! This was not what I wanted to see. Disappointment filled me. Not only did berries pour forth from the bag but so did leaves, tiny twigs, and little stems. What a mess! I did not intend to mix all that into the muffin batter. The delicious possibilities of the fruit were spoiled by all the debris that had been left in the berries. It was a long process at this point to clean away all the leaves and other pieces of miscellaneous tundra from the berries that were wet and sticky.

I am in the habit of cleaning my berries while I pick them. I pour them in a slow stream from my picking bucket into a slightly larger bucket or container and let the wind blow away the chaff, leaves, and twigs from the berries. And ta-da, a bucket of clean berries when I am done.

As I look down at the mess in front of me, questions about the condition of myself begin to pour forth. "Is the fruit of my soul 'clean,' or is it mixed with trash or other unwanted debris? Do I need to pour the fruit of my heart, mind, and soul out before God and let the Holy Spirit blow away the chaff that doesn't belong there? Do I need to give up or let go of some items to be pure in God's sight? What do other people see in my life? Am I saying one thing but living another? Is the fruit of my life causing me to be a stumbling block to another believer?" These are some difficult questions, but they cause me to consider the state of the fruit in my own life.

Let's not allow our witness to be spoiled by fruit that isn't clean. Let's listen and be sensitive and obedient as the Holy Spirit shows us things of this world that we need to let go of so we might produce clean and pure fruit.

> But the fruit of the Spirit is love, joy, peace, patience, kindness, goodness, faithfulness, gentleness and self-control. Against such things there is no law. (Galatians 5:23)

Looking

know just where I am headed today—out to God's garden to that one special place where the berries grow big and fat! I came upon it a couple years ago. It has been a faithful little patch of berries, and it has always rewarded me with a quick two quarts. And out the door I go. I hike down the path and out onto the tundra looking for the landmarks. I arrive, only to face disappointment. Lots of green leaves and healthy-looking bushes, but no berries. I look around to make sure this is where I was last year; yep, same leaning tree with a Y in the trunk. Same little ravine, and right there is the tundra puddle. Yep, this has to be the spot. But why are all the bushes empty of fruit?

Hmmm. I stand there looking around and begin wondering, does God ask that question when He bends down to look at my life and see how the fruit is growing that He has planted and nurtured? Does He wonder where it is? God invests into our lives. He has given us

His holy word, His Holy Spirit, and His promises of faithfulness and provision. He has blessed our lives with people who mentor and disciple us and come alongside us. He has given us a church family or a body of believers. Does He have to stop and look around and say, "Yep, I'm sure I have given the gift of love and forgiveness so it may be given to others. Yet, where is it?" Am I letting the gifts God gives to me overflow so that they produce fruit so I and others may benefit?

In the Arctic, it seems the growth of bountiful berries rotates around a little from place to place and time to time. There is always fruit growing somewhere, but it changes some from year to year, and sometimes I must hunt for it.

I believe it is God's will that we be consistent, showing love and forgiveness, extending kindness and mercy. We are more effective in our ministry and Christian walk if we maintain this consistency by remaining in Him and in His word.

It is my prayer that I would not be a "rotating" berry bush but that I would be faithful to produce fruit from the tender loving care and nurturing that I receive from the Lord.

As the words of Jesus remind us, "I am the vine; you are the branches. If a man remains in me and I in him, he will bear much fruit; apart from me you can do nothing" (John 15:5).

17

In Season

$\mathcal{I}$ flip the calendar to a new month. Time is passing. Seasons are changing. I pause and ponder the fact that life also has its seasons. Childhood moves into teenage years. Teenagers quickly pass to adulthood. There is the season of babies and young children. There is the season of aged parents. There is the season of the empty nest. Even some friendships have seasons; people pass into and then through our lives and bless us for the season they are here.

Fruit also has its season. In Noatak, we know that as soon as the salmon run has come in mid-July, it is time to start checking the blueberries. Blueberries are somewhat of a fragile fruit. The season can be cut short by too much hard rain or strong winds that knock the berries off the bushes. Freezing temperatures can also greatly shorten the life span of the berry by making them soft and mushy. In the arctic, nothing is for certain. Any month can bring freezing temperatures. Fall time is known for gusty, stormy weather. So if we want berries, we get them as soon as we can.

The seasons of our lives offer us the opportunity to bear many different types of fruit for God's kingdom. If we are retired, maybe we can volunteer and make ourselves available to our church to support and work in capacities that need filled. But maybe we are in the busy stages of life with children running around and the best we can do is provide a bag of coffee for the Thursday-morning prayer group. Others may have physical limitations that prevent them from teaching or cooking, but they can lift the prayer needs of the church before the throne of grace.

This is the season to bear fruit, whatever season we find ourselves in at the moment. God knows our hearts, our abilities, and our limitations. He is also able to take whatever we can offer, whatever His grace has nurtured in our hearts, and use it for His glory! So take heart—the fruit we bear is in season!

> Whatever you do, work at it with all your heart, as working for the Lord, not men, since you know that you will receive an in heritance from the Lord as a reward. It is the Lord Christ you are serving. (Col. 3:23–24)

And we pray this in order that you may live a life worthy of the Lord and may please him in every way: bearing fruit in every good work, growing in the knowledge of God. (Col. 1:10)

Brrr. It's Cold!

The snow is three feet deep on the tundra. The thermometer reads -36°. The months of December, January, and February are the coldest and darkest months in the Arctic. Long gone is the warmth of the summer sun. Below the blanket of snow, frozen in the cold, are the blueberry bushes. And there they stay, buried until mid-May when the sun melts the snow and the tundra reappears. Then, in a matter of a couple weeks, blossoms begin to show. It is amazing to think that the plants can survive the harshness of this environment.

You and I live in a harsh environment. This world can often be a cruel place. We are tainted and tormented by sin, our enemy prowling around. We stay in bed with the covers over our heads because we feel we can't stand another day of failure or disappointment. The struggles seem too big, too high. We can't face our boss, the scales, hearing the two-year-old whine again, more bills in the mail, no texts messages on our phone.

Yet, it is God's will for us that we not only survive but thrive. He calls us to bear fruit. If we choose to stand in His grace, He enables us to bear up under our circumstances. As we pull together and pray together, we are strengthened to face our trials. And in doing so, we bear fruit. We reflect our Savior. Others are watching and see us stand firm, stand up, stand. The winds come, the snow flies, our soul shudders in the dark. But God has promised and is faithful, "Never will I leave you. Never will I forsake you" (Heb. 13:5). We wait, we trust, we hope, and we keep holding on.

Then one day, we realize we can feel the warmth of the Son and His grace and love, and it is melting away at the cold around us. There is change. Hope is coming to life. Perseverance is a long, hard word. It is no fun. I'm not talking about the spelling or pronunciation. I'm talking about living it. If we must persevere, it means there is opposition or difficulties.

Persevering. The berry bushes remind me every spring and summer that just as God created them to survive and thrive, He also has made a way for me to survive and thrive—to bear up and bear fruit even in the midst of adverse situations and circumstances.

So do not fear, for I am with you; do not be dismayed, for I am your God. I will strengthen you and help you; I will uphold you with my righteous right hand. (Isaiah 41:10)

Is It Payday?

*H*igh, thin clouds hang like a canopy in the ceiling of the heavens. The day is bright, and the wind is blowing. I call to collect the kids from the four corners of the house. Their response when they hear my plans for the day is nothing but complaints and arguments.

"Awww, Mom."

"Why right now? I am busy reading *Anne of Green Gables*."

"I don't want to pick. There are too many mosquitos."

"I wanted to go fishing this morning."

And on goes the list of pleas and excuses—to no avail. My mind is made up, and the course for the day has been set.

"It's too much work to pick berries. Why can't we just buy some?"

I hear one more rebuttal as the kids trudge down the steps behind me. I ignore it, and we make our way to God's garden. The kids forget their complaining and settle down in various spots to pick berries.

It is work to pick berries. It can be tedious and monotonous. Often, it is hot. In an effort to keep away the pesky bugs, we cover ourselves from head to toe using sweatshirts or *atikluks* (cotton covering with long sleeves and hood) all the way to rubber boots. Some even use white cotton gloves to cover up hands. Our backs become tired from bending and stooping. Work—work that is not rewarded with a paycheck.

I am reminded that much of the work we do for the kingdom of God is very much like this scenario. We drag our feet, offer complaints or resistance. We might even want financial compensation or to pay someone else to do the job. Yes, some churches can offer paid positions for youth leaders or children's workers—even worship leaders. But there is almost always work in the church that God reveals to us or calls us to that doesn't offer monetary compensation, and often the work can seem menial or tedious.

We are no different than the examples we see in scripture, Abraham, Noah, and Mary, to name a few. These all had to perform tedious, menial tasks for God. But we also see that when we obey, as they obeyed, when we do the work God has set before us, as they faithfully completed the work God had placed before them, His kingdom is built, and there is great reward.

When he saw the crowds, he had compassion on them, because they were harassed and helpless, like sheep without a shepherd. Then he said to his disciples, "The harvest is plentiful but the workers are few. Ask the Lord of the harvest, therefore, the send out workers into his harvest field." (Matthew 9:36–38)

Drawing from the Storehouse

Days of endless sunshine, warm temperatures, and breeze. This can describe Arctic summer days (they can also be cold, chilly, and rainy); but often, we do enjoy beautiful summer weather. Of course, it is in this beautiful summer season of endless light when the berries become ripe. I could truly pick nearly 'round the clock if my energy allowed. It is a great time of gathering and reaping, storing and freezing.

The winter is nearly the opposite—days of cold and darkness, especially if it is stormy or cloudy. Not at all berry-picking weather. However, because of our diligence in the summer, we can go to the freezer and pull out a bag of berries and enjoy a bowl of berries, milk, and sugar (a local favorite here in Noatak), or add some berries to muffins or pancake batter. We can spread blueberry jam on our toast during the deep cold of January. We draw from the stores we have put away in the summer months.

It seems our spiritual lives also have seasons—summers and winters. We experience times of great bounty and blessing. God fills us and enriches us, and we soak it up. Our souls are sunny—filled with faith and hope, strength and peace. Prayers are answered. Scripture becomes life in our life. God grows fruit in our inner being—love, joy, peace, patience, kindness, goodness, gentleness, faithfulness, and self-control.

Then days of darkness arrive. Life takes staggering swings at us in the form of the loss of loved ones, grief of a wayward child, loss of health, and disappointment in a failed marriage. There are even circumstances that aren't so life-shattering—a missed job promotion, minor health issues, a betrayal. The enemy comes swinging, but God has equipped our hearts and stands by us ready to pour out His grace to us in our winter months.

Growth may be gone, but the fruit remains. The sun may not be shining, but we have put away His fruit in the storehouses of our hearts. It is there. He can give us forgiveness for betrayal, mental and emotional strength in our time of physical weakness, and a prodigal love for a wayward child. We have walked with Him in the summer months, and our souls are filled with promises and hope. And in the winter we open the doors of the storehouses of our soul and draw from His fruit, and we are sustained by His continued grace and love.

I have told you these things, so that in me you may have peace. In this world you will have trouble. But take heart! I have over come the world. (John 16:33)

Are You Busy?

$\mathcal{I}$ have a to-do list hanging on the side of the fridge. It is never done. Throughout the day I cross off items that have been accomplished. At the end of the day, the items left on the list become part of my list for the next day. Laundry, phone calls, items to mail, papers to fill out, children to babysit, bread to bake, dishes, meetings, and Sunday school papers to sort. The list is really endless.

The item that will be added to the list for the next several weeks is berry picking. Time consuming. Some days it is all-consuming. Yet the other items on my to-do list don't disappear. But I know I have to make the sacrifice if I want the reward of berries in my freezer for the winter months.

Christian service seems to parallel this same idea. There is always enough for any of us to do on any given day. Yet in the midst of all our daily obligations, there are prayer needs and lessons to study. Someone needs a listening ear, a shoulder to cry on. And it takes time. We are faced with the daily choice of how we will spend our time.

We sacrifice our time for the sake of the kingdom. During berry season, the sacrifice of time is made from daily obligations and responsibilities to provide and prepare for the winter months. So it is with our spiritual lives. Seasons come when we sacrifice our time—give up our daily obligations to care for the needs of God's people and invest in the eternal kingdom.

The phone rings. "Are you busy? Do you have a minute?" I hear the waver in the voice of the person on the other end of the line. I look at the dishes in the sink, the clean clothes waiting on the couch to be folded, the bread dough rounding in the bowl under the dishtowel on the counter. I have a decision to make. Am I willing to give up not just a minute, but thirty minutes to this hurting troubled soul who is in need of a listening ear and a prayer?

During berry season, I am willing to put my to-do list aside to take care of what really matters in that season of life. How much more should I be willing to lay aside my to-do list and take care of heart matters—eternal matters?

> As God's fellow workers we urge you not
> to receive God's grace in vain. For he says,

"In the time of my favor I heard you, and in the day of salvation I helped you." I tell you, now is the time of God's favor, now is the day of salvation. (2 Cor. 6:1–2)

Plumping Up

$\mathcal{H}$ere I am again, enjoying the pleasure of entering God's bountiful garden. It is peaceful. The ravens fly here and there, squawking and cawing above me in the sky. I hear the call of the cranes coming across the tundra. The seagulls call to each other. I take a deep breath, recognizing the beauty and perfection in the creation of my almighty God.

My focus turns to my purpose at hand. I look at the bushes around me. I see berries. I stoop to begin picking. The berries are smallish. I pick a few and move on. More small berries. I scoop a few more berries off the branches, enjoying the cool feeling of the berries as they roll onto my fingers, picking and walking. I am hoping to be rewarded with some nice-sized berries. After a while, I realize I must return home to begin dinner for my family. I was not successful in finding the big berries I was after.

The next day, there is rain, and then more rain, and

my picking efforts are delayed for a couple days. Then the weather clears, and I make my way out to the blueberry patch again. But this time the scene is different. Even though I am in the same patch as before, the berries are plump and full and sweet to taste.

Sometimes the fruit in my life is small. Maybe it is the smallness of my effort or zeal or faith or prayers. And inevitably, trials come. The rains fall. I stand resigned to my circumstances. But in my situation, I choose to lift my face to God. The rains pour down, but my prayers go up. Then one day, a dear friend reminds me of the promise of God's everlasting love from the word of God. The pastor speaks a message about the armor of God and using the shield of faith. There is prayer, and somehow, there is faith. And I am enabled to stand.

The weather clears. The trial passes. The dampness of the clouds is replaced by the warmth of the Son. My faith has grown, the prayers become consistent, and I stand on the word of God with the shield of faith in my hand. The fruit in my life has become sweeter. God's grace flows more strongly in my life and out to others. Experiencing hardship or turmoil by way of trials and testing grows in me the ability to understand and pray for others who also face similar situations.

And I am thankful for the results of the rain. The berries are perfectly plump and delicious. So also may the fruit in my life, even as a result of difficulties and troubles, produce a grace that is pleasing and sweet to others and glorifies the kingdom of God.

> Praise be to the God and Father of our Lord Jesus Christ, the Father of compassion and the God of all comfort, who comforts us in all our troubles, so that we can comfort those in any trouble with the comfort we ourselves have received from God. (2 Corinthians 1:3–5)

Keep Reaching

"Oooooo," I groan under my breath. I stand and rub my lower back for a minute, trying to relieve a little of the ache and tightness that is there from bending and stooping most of the afternoon. Complaining thoughts crouch at the edge of my mind—thoughts about wishing the bushes weren't so low and the tundra wasn't so wet and lumpy. I immediately correct my thinking to a thankful attitude of gratitude for all God's freely given provisions. My only responsibility is the picking. He has provided the land and done the planting and the watering. I smile in thankfulness and stoop again to pick, surrendering to the task at hand.

As I pick, I am reminded that God also has a spiritual harvest field—a harvest field that is in need of workers. And I wonder about my posture. Am I bent, surrendered, and obedient to the way God wants to use me in "harvesting" for Him? Am I willing to bear up under the weight of working for His kingdom?

I think about my motions of picking: looking, bending, stooping, reaching. Bending before God. Bending in submission and surrender. Bending in repentance. Bending in worship and prayer. Looking for what God has for me. Looking for the place where I can use the gifts and talents He has bestowed upon me that they might be used for His glory. Stooping low, having a servant's heart. Stooping to make the effort. Stooping even if no one notices. And reaching. Reaching to others. Others who need teaching, hugging, visiting, friendship, time, love, forgiveness. Reaching requires openness and willingness. Reaching requires action and obedience.

Another handful of berries plop into my almost-full bucket. My back is tired and sore, but come this winter, it will be worth the effort. In the same way, our efforts for God's kingdom, although tiring and difficult in this present life, are reaping an eternal reward. It is a harvest of souls that will remain for all eternity—lives that have been changed for Jesus. It is a harvest that leaves no room for regrets or remembers the struggles and difficulties. It is a harvest that rejoices with thankfulness for the efforts given by the workers. We are those workers.

> For we are God's fellow workers; you are God's field, God's building. (1 Corinthians 3:9)

Let Go

"The fruit looks ripe," I mumble to myself from the middle of the patch as I check to see if the berries are ripe. I look around and see little blue specks peeking out from under green leaves. I bend down to pick some from the blueberry stems. "Hmmmm"—not coming off easily. I taste one of the berries in my hand. "Wow"—still a little tart. But I reason to myself that even if these berries are still a little sour, they will be fine in baking muffins or coffee cake. I continue to pick and pluck, but the berries don't really want to let go of the stems. It requires a little more effort on my part, but I keep at it.

As I continue picking at the blueberry bushes, I am wondering about the fruit in my life. Am I holding on to my fruit? Am I clutching to myself the things God is growing in my heart and life? Do I want to "show off" my fruit but not let go of it so that it may bless and feed others?

Sharing fruit requires a "letting go," a giving up, or a turning-over process. The bush shares its fruit with me. I did nothing to aid the process of growth. It owes me nothing, yet the berry bush surrenders its fruit to my hand. Is it the same with me?

God is at work growing fruit in my life—knowledge, skills, talents, gifts, grace, love, and forgiveness. But these have no value if I am unwilling to share, let go, release, or hold these out to others that they may be fed. Some may grab, use, take advantage of, or not appreciate this fruit. But the fruit is not mine to hold on to. It is up to God to use what He has grown in my life for His kingdom. I am the vessel through which it has been grown. But I am not the owner. I must release it to be used for God's glory.

I pull a few more berries free of the stems and wonder if God is having to tug at me and my life or if I am freely and willingly releasing His fruit that it may produce a harvest of righteousness.

> Let us not become weary in doing good, for at the proper time we will reap a harvest if we do not give up. Therefore, as we have opportunity, let us do good to all people, especially to those who belong to the family of believers. (Galatians 6:9–10)

Blueberries Anyone?

I'm sitting downstairs on the couch sewing, enjoying the dark Arctic evenings of quiet productivity when it is all interrupted by clamoring feet on the stairs and the eruption of the question, "Mom, what can I have for a snack?" My four teenage kids are asking me again. It's only been two hours since dinner, but bedtime is around the corner. I wonder if they can really be hungry—again? "Can we have blueberries, milk, and sugar?" they beg me. I see their pleading eyes.

"Let me see how many berries there are left in the freezer." I get up and walk out to the freezer. It is mid-January, and I want to make sure I will have enough to last through the winter. I take inventory and decide there is enough for them to have berries this time. Between the four of them, they can nearly eat a whole gallon of berries in one sitting, so tonight I limit them each to one bowl.

I return to my sewing and hear the frozen berries

plinking into the bowls and think about the hard work in providing for the winter. I'm sitting there thinking that all my hard work is just getting eaten up … But then I stop myself in mid-thought and laugh at my thinking. "Isn't this exactly what all that picking was for: eating, sharing, and enjoying?" I smile to myself, and my heart is happy that my children are enjoying the fruits of my summer labor.

Sharing. It would be no good to my family or others if I picked all the berries and just kept them in the freezer all winter long without using them. How silly to open the freezer in June to have ten gallons of blueberries still sitting there. I am only blessed if the berries are shared and used.

I am reminded that as God blesses me in my life, it only becomes a complete blessing when I pass it on to others in some way or form. God has forgiven me my sins, but it is only in me extending forgiveness to others that God is glorified. His life shines in me. It is the same with love. God loves me. But when I give that love to others, they are able to see the beauty of God—His work in my heart. This principle is true for most of our life. God gives to us; he blesses us, not so we can have but so we can give to others what we have been freely given. It is in the giving and sharing and passing on to others that God is magnified and others can clearly see Him.

So, yes. Enjoy a bowl of blueberries, milk, and sugar.

Do not judge, and you will not be judged. Do not condemn, and you will not be condemned. Forgive, and you will be forgiven. Give, and it will be given to you. A good measure, pressed down, shaken together and running over, will be poured into your lap. For with the measure you use, it will be measured to you. (Luke 6:37–38)

Where Is the Fruit?

"Let's stop there." I speak above the noise of the boat motor as I motion to my husband. We are out looking for good blueberry patches along the river. I want to stop and check the ridge ahead for berries. He slows the boat, and we ease up to the bank. I grab the anchor and jump out. After the anchor is shoved into the gravel at the edge of the river, I clamber up the side of the bank. There are lots of green, beautiful berry bushes. I begin looking, only to be disappointed. There are no berries! I look deeper into the bushes and push the branches around. Nope. Nothing. How can there be so many berry bushes yet be so empty? No fruit?

Our churches suffer when we grow as Christians, yet fail to produce fruit. As believers, we must be transformed and renewed in our minds and our beings. With renewal comes growth and fruit. As the Holy Spirit transforms our minds, we are able to give up old habits and replace them with godly practices.

I was a busy mother of four children, ages newborn to five and a half. I was tired. It was easy to become careless, and I had started letting my emotions get the upper hand. Yelling quickly became my method of discipline. The Holy Spirit reminded me that yelling out of anger and tiredness was not pleasing to Him, nor was it a good example to my children. Through time, prayer, and practice, God helped me give up harshness and trade it for love. But it all came from me seeking forgiveness and asking Him for grace and wisdom that could only come from God.

Growing spiritual fruit requires letting the Holy Spirit show us what we are lacking or what we need to get rid of or let go of. Many times, this isn't easy. It isn't what is comfortable, and we are tempted to keep holding on to our old habits and thought patterns. As Christians, it isn't easy to admit that we are falling short of how God wants us to live. It takes humility to admit, "Yes, I need God to help me get rid of this or let go of that. And Lord, let the fruit of the Spirit grow in my life."

But when we are willing to humble ourselves and take that step, God's grace begins to flow in our lives, and spiritual fruit begins to grow and replace old habits. We are no longer empty bushes. We begin to bear fruit—fruit that will last. Fruit that has eternal value. Fruit that bears witness to whose we are. Fruit that supports our church families and brings encouragement to others. Let us be fruit-bearing bushes for the kingdom of God.

> You did not choose me, but I chose you and appointed you to go and bear fruit— fruit that will last. (John 15:14)

> This is to my father's glory, that you bear much fruit, showing yourselves to be my disciples. (John 15:8)

Little Is Much

I see the berries from way over. Lots of blue grabbed my eyes' attention. I sloshed through the mucky tundra grass to the edge of the trees. Sure enough, lots of blueberries, little blueberries. My heart feels disappointment, but I can't resist picking because there are so many berries. I begin to run my fingers over the stems and pull the berries into my hand, then let them roll into the bucket. So small. I decide to taste them. I am surprised at how big the flavor is in spite of the size of the berry. I continue to pick because the flavor is so yummy.

As I pick, God begins to open my mind, and thoughts begin to flow about the size of fruit in our lives as Christians. What determines how "big" or grand our fruit is? Do I possess a lesser value if my fruit is considered "small" by others? Who created me the way I am? Who has given me the talents I have? Who made that blueberry bush with such small berries? Why don't all the bushes produce large, marble-sized fruit?

I began to ponder and think and ask God His thoughts. He didn't really give me a straight answer except these thoughts. Fruit is fruit, small or big. It has nutritional value. It contains sustenance. That berry bush is doing the job God has given it to do. Even if it is producing small fruit according to my standards, it is still fulfilling its purpose. No matter how small it may seem to others, when God is in it, it is enough. And it fills my bucket.

Lord, forgive me when I think the task You ask me to do is too small. Help me to trust that whatever You have given me to do has a purpose. And I do not have a lesser value because my job seems smaller. If it is used for Your glory and is fulfilling Your purpose, then it is not insignificant. Help me to be faithful to live and be what Your will is for my life. May I live and walk in obedience to You.

And I was reminded of the young boy among the crowd of five thousand who only had five loaves and two small fish, yet he was willing to give what he had. And Jesus took it and blessed it and the multitude was fed! Nothing is too small for Jesus to multiply.

> He replied, "you give them something to eat." They answered, "we have only five loaves of bread and two fish." ... Then

taking the five loaves and the two fish and looking up to heaven, he gave thanks and broke them ... they all ate and were satisfied, and the disciples picked up twelve basketfuls of broken pieces that were left over. (Luke 9:13–17)

Beyond Life

Arigaa (an Iñupiaq word for deep contentment or happiness). The berry season has ended, and my freezer is happy. Stacked neatly in one corner is my family's winter supply of berries. We live in a culture where many families rely heavily on subsistence—gathering and living from what the land, river, and ocean provide. Blueberries are one of these provisions.

The frosts have come, and the ground is mostly frozen; however, it is not covered with snow. The leaves have been drained of their fall beauty, dried and fallen to the ground. As I walk across the tundra, I am amazed at what I see; hundreds of blueberries still clinging to bare branches! "What?" I ask myself. "How can this be? How could the many berry pickers that flooded the tundra just a few weeks ago miss all these berries?" The fallen leaves reveal the fruit.

It is true in our lives. We are human. We are going

to pass from this present world and leave this life behind. The green of our lives turns into a beautiful autumn, and then one day the presence of God blows across our souls, and we are gathered to Him. All that is left on this earth is a dry, withered body. But there is the fruit still clinging! What hope! What joy! What encouragement!

In Christ, we possess the ability to bear fruit that lasts beyond our life span here on earth! In the absence of our physical body, our spiritual life and the fruit that God grew in us can still be evident to others. My grandmother was this kind of lady. Her example and lifestyle are still remembered; her wisdom is still alive in my mind. Her prayers are still present before the throne of grace. Her fruit is still living and producing more fruit! In me. In others.

The branches are nearly bare. Most of the leaves are fallen or blown away. But the fruit is still there, even in the absence of the fullness of life of the berry bush.

> Lord, may I produce a fruit in my life that will stand the test of time, and even after this physical life is gone, may the fruit that has been grown by You in my heart and of my hands make a difference in eternity.

> You did not choose me, but I chose you and appointed you to go and bear fruit— fruit that will last. (John 14:16)

Have Patience

*T*ime. Never enough time. It's a priceless commodity. We all have the same allotment of time each day; twenty-four hours, and the freedom to choose how we will use this gift. We can't hold onto time. We can't stop it. We can only live in each moment and allow these moments that turn to minutes, then hours and days, months and years, and eventually a life to be fruitful for Christ.

The berry season has reached its peak, and the berries seem to be perfectly ripe—perfectly sweet and firm. And I'm thinking about time—becoming ripe. How pleasing and wonderful to experience the taste of a perfectly ripe berry. And I'm thinking about the waiting process involved. Time. Patience.

In the spring, the blueberries don't sprout berries. They sprout blossoms. And over time the fruit appears and develops and ripens. This same process is true in our lives. As Christians, our conversion trip to the altar

Doris Van Amburg

(or wherever this happened in our lives) was just the beginning of our blooming, growing, and ripening. It can be dangerous and very disheartening for us if we are looking around at others, wondering why we are not at the same place in our journey with Christ as they are. If we are looking at the Christian sitting across the aisle from us in church, thinking he or she has the perfect fruit, thinking our own fruit is nonexistent or inferior to them, we are putting ourselves in a dangerous situation.

It is important that we keep our eyes focused on Jesus and His word and not on others around us. As God's children, we are all at different places in our spiritual journey with God. We all started our journey with Christ at different stages in life. God is faithful and will bring our lives into perfection as we continue to look to Him and to His word for guidance. As we are faithful to walk in step with the Spirit and live in obedience to God, our fruit will grow and ripen to completion and perfectness. Just as the flavor of the blueberry grows sweeter with time, so we too will develop a sweet spirit that Christ grows in us—if we will be patient and keep growing.

Give God time. We are a work in progress, and God's work comes with a promise.

> Being confident of this, that he who began a good work in you will carry it on to completion until the day of Christ Jesus. (Philippians 1:6)

Lighten the Load

My family loves to eat berries, and not just when they are in season, but all winter long. We have a family of six, which includes four growing teens or preteens. It would be nearly impossible for myself alone to pick enough berries to last our family through the winter (at least the way my kids like to eat them). So I have enlisted my children to join in the picking. They each have their quota to pick according to their age. It is a huge help to have them join in the efforts to gather berries for our family. It lightens my load tremendously. I am very thankful for their contribution.

As Christians, we are at work in the harvest field for the Lord. He is in need of workers no matter their age or experience. There is something that each and every one of us can do. As we make our contribution, it lightens the load that someone else is carrying.

Sometimes I hear complaints and whining from my

children. They don't want to spend the morning getting hot and sweaty and swatting mosquitos and gnats to pick berries. It is hard work. No fun. They enjoy going to the freezer and pulling out a gallon bag and pouring some into a bowl for a snack. But they don't enjoy the work.

And I'm thinking about myself. Do I ever complain about following through on the work God asks of me? Do I say things like, "Why do I have to do this? I'm the one who did this last time." Or, "They always call me to do such and such. Why can't so and so do it this time?" Am I a faithful worker in God's harvest field? I enjoy certain programs the church offers; children's church, Sunday school, nursery, Bible study. I also enjoy a clean sanctuary, coffee, and rolls during fellowship time. But am I willing to do my part in the church body?

"Many hands make light work." This is true in the blueberry patch, and it is true in the church body. May I be faithful to God in doing my part—pitching in to lift the load and helping to carry the burden of the work of the church so that the workers may be plentiful in the harvest field of righteousness.

> So we rebuilt the wall till all of it reached
> half its height, for the people worked with
> all their heart. (Neh. 4:6)

Bzzzzzzz

I reach in the clump of willows to pick the plump, ripe berries that are waiting there. *Zzzzzzzz* is followed by a smack. One more dead mosquito. I pluck at the berries and hear the continued buzzing in my ears. I stand and try to catch a hint of some breeze to help blow away the nasty pests and give me reprieve, but to no avail. I continue to reach and pick and try to shut out the buzzing that encompasses the air all around me. I try to focus on something, anything besides the droning of the incessant hum of the mosquitos. But my thoughts keep getting drowned in the persistent thrum of these hovering little creatures. I keep moving and picking, and they aren't brave enough to land. I don't stay still long enough to give them a chance to bite. But the noise in my ears bothers me to no end! I look in my bucket and decide this is enough for today and begin my journey back across the tundra to the trail that leads to my home.

Victory. I'm disgusted. Those little pests, as small as they are, were successful in driving me from my task. The berries are ready to be picked but the pesky insects were too much for me. I want to turn back and continue picking, but my mind needs a break from the constant droning.

As I am trudging and sloshing back across the tundra in defeat, I am thinking. Wondering. How am I doing with the work that God has set before me; teaching Sunday school, leading worship, praying, praising, raising my family, or caring for a family member who is sick? Am I letting myself be defeated by little annoying thoughts that come to my mind? Do I allow the enemy to flood my heart with doubts or fears about what God has placed in my hand to do?

Mosquitos are large in Alaska, but they are still a small insect. There is a statistic that states that, per pound, mosquitos outnumber moose! I don't know if it is true or how they came to that conclusion, but it is amazing to think about! Comparatively, mosquitos are tiny compared to moose. Yet it is this small creature that has driven me from the blueberry patch, not the moose.

I believe we have an enemy who uses the tactic of placing ever so small thoughts, doubts, and fears in our minds, and he does this over and over until we feel oppressed with the burden of them. And we give up; we give in. We quit the work that is at hand, even though we see the need and sense the burden—even though we see the children and their pleading eyes. We allow the hum and buzz of little thoughts placed by the enemy to drown out the needs of God's harvest field.

Lord, help me to stand. Help me to put on the whole armor of God. Help me to recognize the enemy and to resist him. Help me to move forward with what You have given me to accomplish for your eternal kingdom. Amen.

> Then the Lord said to him, "Who gave man his mouth? Who makes him deaf or mute? Who gives him sight or makes him blind? Is it not I, the Lord? Now go; I will help you speak and teach you what to say." (Exodus 4:11–12)

Here's How

"Hello." I answer the phone. I hear my friend's voice on the other end asking me if I can make it out this morning to go picking. I glance around at a sink full of dishes and a toddler in training pants and a baby in diapers.

"Let me check with my husband." I check, and he gives me the go ahead. My friend will pick me up in ten minutes. I gather my buckets, a water bottle, and a granola bar and put them in my backpack, along with some paper towels and bug dope.

I am new in Noatak. I don't really know anybody except my husband. He has lived here for several years and has many good friends. Thankfully, his friends are willing to accept me too. But there is still the awkwardness of being new—not knowing about proper customs and how things are done.

But this morning, I am off to the berry patch with

a newly forming friendship. I feel happy and eager to be going out, gathering, and learning. She shows me places to pick. I learn how to pour my berries from one container to another and let the wind winnow the sticks, bugs, and leaves from the fruit so I have a clean bucket of berries to take home. I watch and learn subtle things about better berry picking—what to wear, what not to wear, how many, and what size buckets to bring. I learn about wearing a covering over my head to keep the hair off my face and bugs out of my ears, and other little things. These are common sense to the Iñupiaq who have grown up picking berries on the tundra. But for this farm girl from the Midwest, it is a whole different ball game!

These days, I'm somewhat savvy when it comes to picking. I know the ropes, and I am comfortable hiking myself out onto the tundra. I feel competent about being able to pick. But all the thanks go to that first friend who was willing to come alongside and teach me the tricks of the trade.

The harvest field of ministry is very similar to this same scenario. In our churches there are young Christians and new members who are willing and eager to work for the Lord. But they need someone to come alongside them and show them the ropes, someone to help them feel comfortable learning a new role. Hopefully, those of us in church bodies who are seasoned and equipped are willing to pass on the baton of knowledge, wisdom, and instruction—that we would be those who would teach and mentor from a loving heart.

It takes time to build relationships with others, especially those from a different culture or generation. But we are all a part of the family of God. I want to be willing to partner up with others. I want to be willing to pass along wisdom, knowledge, and understanding that others were willing to pass on to me, not just in the berry patch, but in the ministry of the church. I want to come alongside and give of my time to teach and mentor in the same way others gave to me.

Lord, let my eyes see those You would call me to team up with so that Your kingdom may be strengthened and continue to grow and be built up for Your name's sake.

> Dear children, let us not love with words
> or tongue but with actions and in truth.
> (1 John 3:18)

Sharing

I'm picking. My bucket is filling. I'm enjoying my time in God's garden, feeling deep thankfulness in the bounty of His provision again. My heart feels full, and I smile. God is blessing me with strength and time and the ability to gather. As I pick, I wonder which elder also needs a share in this blessing? A few names come to mind.

I remain there, reaping the bounty of the tundra and pondering about my life and my heart and enjoy the afternoon of picking until I reach the amount of berries I had set out to get, making sure I picked enough to give some away. I finish winnowing the berries and head home to put them into baggies to store away for the winter. I put my quota in the freezer and grab the bag designated to give away from the countertop. I put the Ziploc full of berries in a plastic store bag and head out the door to start the Honda (generic term used for any ATV). I head off to make my delivery to one of the elderly ladies who can no longer make it to the berry patch to pick. I knock on the door and let myself in. She is sitting in her same red chair. I smile and tell her I was thinking of her. She smiles and responds, "*Yoi. Taikuu.*" These are the Inupiaq words that would translate into English something like, "Lucky, wow, thank you." She motions with her eyes toward the fridge. I see this communication and understand her. I know that means she wants me to put them in her freezer over there, so I walk over, open the door, and tuck them in.

I sit down in my same spot on the couch across from her and wait. She begins talking, sharing about God's faithfulness to her—His healing touch on her life and in her body. She has me look at a verse from the Bible and we discuss it briefly. Her heart is overflowing with thankfulness for what God has done in her life. And there in the quiet of the afternoon, there is fellowship—a sharing of fruit. I walked through her door intending to share the fruit of my labor that day. But I left with a fed spirit because she shared the fruit of the word and spoke of God's fruit in her life.

What a blessing to be joined in a circle of friends who share the fruit of what God has done and is continuing to do in their lives. Sharing this kind of spiritual fruit has an eternal effect on lives and souls. This day I am reminded to be faithful to pass on and share with others the words and works of the Father, the Son, and the Spirit in my life. Just as sharing the berries provides physical sustenance, so sharing the fruit of a testimony, an answered prayer, or a promise from scripture produces an eternal, spiritual sustenance.

> Therefore encourage one another and build each other up, just as in fact you are doing. (1 Thessalonians 4:7)

Living with Bears

We live in an isolated Iñupiaq village about seventy-five miles north of the Arctic Circle. Our house is the last house at the edge of the village on the north end of town. We literally live on the edge of the whole northern slope of Alaska, right in the middle of all the wild, roaming arctic animal. I have seen caribou, wolves, and moose from my living room window and have had muddy bear claw streaks smudging down the outside of the dining room window. There are wild things out there!

The fact remains, however, that me and many other people brave the wilds—the potential dangers of the berry patch to pick every year. I could stay home and shudder in fear. I could let the reality of what might be lurking in the willows keep me from blessing my family and others with provisions for the winter months. But I choose to pray a prayer of protection and walk out and face the wild.

It occurred to me that as Christians, we face a very similar situation. There is work to be done for the kingdom of God. There are places of service where God can use our hands and feet and voice. It seems to so happen that these places can often be on the edge of wild. They are far away from the familiar, or they really are in areas of danger or risk. These places may be in a country far away, on a sidewalk across town, in a pew at church, or even within our own homes. Any time we take a stand or make a stand for truth, for Christ, we have forged an enemy: Satan.

The word of God reminds us in 1 Peter 5:8 that we have an enemy who "prowls around like a roaring lion looking for someone to devour." But we are reminded in 1 John 4:4, "Greater is He that is in us than he that is in the world." Yes, we have an enemy, but he is a defeated enemy. No matter how scary the thoughts are that he shoots at our minds, they are empty threats. "If God is for us, who can be against us?" (Rom. 8:31).

I don't want the possibility of bears to keep me out of the berry patch. I'm not willing to let fear stop me from picking what God has grown and so freely given. Let us not give in or give up because of fear of what might be out there. Let us answer the call of obedience to work in the harvest fields of righteousness for God's eternal glory. Let us stand boldly, knowing that God is on our side and whatever he wills to be accomplished will be done.

> For it is God who works in you to will
> and to act according to his good purpose.
> (Philippians 2:13)

What You Got On?

I slip my atikluk over my cotton T-shirt and replace my regular socks with moisture-wicking socks. I pull my hair back tightly into a braid at the base of my neck and put my headband on so that my forehead and ears are mostly covered. I stuff a couple tissues into my pocket and pull on my knee boots. Then I grab my backpack from the hook. It is mostly ready to go, with paper towel, bug dope, a granola bar, and my extra buckets. I just need to put in my water bottle. I slip my sunglasses on my face and head out to pick for the day. I should be prepared for anything.

It took a few years of suffering the bugs, wind, thirst, and other basic human needs before I learned to be fully prepared for several hours of picking. I learned some hard lessons by trial and error (mostly by error) and by tips and pointers from a couple of picking partners. I am a more effective berry picker if I am properly prepared and properly clothed.

On the tundra, there are certain obstacles that can prevent us from accomplishing picking berries; such as, large tundra puddles, so we wear water boots. There are mosquitos and gnats, so we wear something over our head and arms. We bring bug dope to ward off the mosquitos that are too persistent. And a few other items that ease discomfort, like a cool drink of water from the water bottle.

I was feeling grateful for all my proper gear and equipment, as simple as they are. As I was basking in this attitude, God brought to mind the fact that He also has provided proper protection and equipment for us as Christians. We face obstacles in our Christian walk—obstacles that try to bring discouragement to our minds, fear to our hearts. These obstacles might include temptations to lead our feet astray or circumstances that threaten to shatter our faith.

But God's word reminds us that He has provided us with a belt of truth to help defend against doubt and fear, a helmet of salvation to guard our mind, the breastplate of righteousness to protect our hearts, and shoes to lead us in the path of peace. We are also provided with weapons, one being a shield of faith, the gift of being able to believe even if we can't see. And the other is a sword—not just any sword, but the sword of the Spirit, which is the living, holy, true word of God. We are equipped. It is up to us to begin learning to use this equipment so we can live effective and protected for the Lord.

> Therefore put on the full armor of God, so that when the day of evil comes, you may be able to stand your ground, and after you have done everything, to stand. (Ephesians 6:13)

> And may the God of peace ... equip you with everything good for doing his will, and may he work in us what is pleasing to him, though Jesus Christ, to whom be glory for ever and ever. Amen. (Hebrew 13:20–21)

One Goal

I was picking the other day, and I noticed something that was interesting to me, and it began sparking thoughts and connections in my mind. It was a beautiful day. I was picking up on a high cut bank on the edge of the river. The seagulls were calling, and the river was in a hurry to go somewhere, but I was relaxed and focused on plucking those little berries and placing them in my bucket.

It came to my attention that the berry bushes were not even close to being uniform in size or shape. I caught myself pulling nice, plump berries off of a tiny twig, maybe only three or four inches in height. Then, a few minutes later, I was standing picking lots of smallish berries from a big, bushy plant that was maybe eighteen inches tall. Wow! What a difference. Why the variety? It was the same general location with the same amount of sun, wind, rain and temperature. The wheels in my mind began rolling these thoughts around. I wondered if some of the bushes were younger and therefore smaller. But it seemed interesting to me that the bushes, even in their smallness, could produce such beautiful fruit.

I thought about church on Sunday morning. Same building, same songs, same word of God received by our hearts. Some members are elderly and mature, some are young and zealous, and all are producing fruit. God is working in each one, and the work is evident and is manifesting itself by the fruit of our lives.

I wonder if I am tempted to bypass or overlook fruit of the young or the elderly, somehow discrediting it or maybe not understanding it or maybe not willing to take the time to connect with another generation? Heaven forbid and forgive me if this is true.

No matter our age, young or old or somewhere in between, if we are grounded in Christ and soaking up His word, the Holy Spirit is producing fruit in our lives—fruit that is evidence of Christ; fruit that God has plans of using to grow His kingdom; fruit that is holy.

I am willing to reach and pluck the berries off the tiny plants. I am willing to accept the fruit grown by the large, mature plants. It all provides pleasure and nourishment for our bodies. May God help us as a church body to accept and enjoy the fruit that is grown by Him in each and every one of His children. It all has one single purpose—to bring glory to God.

Do not let anyone look down on you because you are young, but set an example for the believers in speech, in life, in love, in faith and in purity. (1 Timothy 4:12)

Growing Up

As my children grew older, I expected more from them. With maturity came responsibility. This expectation extended to the berry patch. I would set a quota for each of them, which I felt was age appropriate. They would have a gallon Ziploc bag with their name on it and they would work towards filling that bag and so on. Needless to say, berry picking was not on the list of their top ten favorite things to do. So, in order not to burn them out on the chore, at the peak of the berry season, I designated berry picking for an hour a day for a week or until their quota was satisfied.

I would be picking along and hear a call come across the tundra: "How much longer, Mom?" Then a few more minutes would pass, and another child would be asking, "Is it time to go yet?" I would do my best to make the task as pleasant as possible, provide a special snack or a bottle of juice, maybe even a soda after they had returned home hot and sweaty. It can be a challenge to balance the mundane chore of picking berries with a seemingly big enough incentive, especially for eight- to twelve-year-old kids. They tend to lose the big picture of the rewards that will await them midwinter if they persevere.

My responsibilities in the church can often seem mundane; same ol', same ol'. I might feel unappreciated or start asking myself questions like, "Why do I have to sit in the nursery again this year?" or "Why can't someone else shovel the walk?" or "Why am I …?" Or whatever the situation may be. We begin to look at ourselves and what we are doing and grumble. It is easy to lose sight of the eternal impact of what we do, our involvement in the body of Christ.

I have been guilty of this, but then the Holy Spirit convicted my heart and I was reminded of several things: that it was my heavenly Father that I worked for, my motive should be love from a servant's heart, and the rewards of obedience and selflessness have eternal dividends. And my perspective was changed. I asked for forgiveness and let God's joy replace my attitude of mundaneness.

As we grow in our spiritual maturity, so we must grow in our work for the kingdom. The berries are out there, but we must go get them. My children are always happy to enjoy berries during the cold, dark months of winter. The harvest is there, but we must reap. The soil is ready, but we must sow. And the reward is eternal. The fruit that we plant, nurture, and reap lasts forever. God has chosen us to be a part of that great harvest field.

Let us remain faithful. Let us persevere. Let us remember who we are really serving.

> She said, "Please let me glean and gather among the sheaves behind the harvesters." She went into the field and has worked steadily from morning till now, except for a short rest in the shelter. (Ruth 2:7)

Keeping Perspective

The tundra where I live is a boundless space without roads or telephone poles. There are no buildings, other than our village, or other manmade landmarks across most of it. Occasionally along the river there will be a cabin; but otherwise, the tundra is covered with low willows and a few black spruce trees that dot the terrain. The hills and mountains become the landmarks and points of guidance.

When I pick berries, my focus is mainly down; my eyes are looking down at the bushes for signs of berries. My feet follow my eyes and hands. I look down and reach and pick and shuffle my feet and move and pick. I kneel down and reach into the willows to pick from the bushes growing there. While I am in that position, I look across into another willow and see more fruit. I scooch over to get in reach and pick some more. If I continue in this pattern too long, there is a chance that when I stand to my feet and look up, I will be disoriented. I will have lost my bearings. It can give my heart a little bit of a start to stop picking, look up, and realize I'm not sure of my location.

I have learned to discipline myself as I pick to look up on a regular basis—to keep a specific pine tree in view and be aware of my position in relation to the mountain in the distance. This keeps me from becoming disoriented, and it makes me feel safe.

I think there is a lesson for us in this as Christians. Is it possible for us to look down too much or to have too narrow of a focus or perspective? As I pick berries, I am looking at what is right there in front of me. And on one hand, that is good. I am focused on my goal. But as I pursue that goal, I must also keep the big picture in mind.

As a part of the body of Christ, I have a specific role or talent that God has given me to use for His kingdom. But I think it is important as I fulfill this role, that I keep in mind the big picture of ministry—of the church, community, and world. I need to work under the umbrella of unity and love and not get so carried away in what I am doing that I miss fitting in with the whole—the big picture.

David reminds us in the psalms of a similar example of perspective. The Israelites would build altars to false idols and gods on the top of the hills and mountains. But David is looking beyond this when he says, "I lift my eyes to the hills—where does my help come from? My help

comes from the Lord, the Maker of heaven and earth"
(Psalm 121:1).

Lord, help me lift my eyes beyond the current situation
I am involved in, whether good or bad; easy or difficult.
Help me continue to be faithful to work where You have
placed me, but to look beyond the details of each day. I
want to keep a proper perspective by keeping my eyes on
You. Amen.

> Let us fix our eyes on Jesus, the author
> and perfecter of our faith, who for the joy
> set before him endured the cross, scorning
> its shame, and sat down at the right had of
> the throne of God. (Hebrews 12:2)

Ready, Set, Go

I have heard the statement that the Arctic has only two seasons, summer and winter. I chuckle at the thought and understand why some may think that. But for those of us who live life above the Arctic Circle, we definitely recognize all four seasons. Winter, of course, is colder and darker than the rest of the year. Spring can still have very cold temperatures, but the Arctic becomes flooded with twenty-four hours of light. Starting in March, we have light nearly all our waking hours. Summer brings even more light, bugs, and warmth—pretty much in that order. Fall begins in late July or early August with cooler temperatures, more rain, more bugs, berries, and the salmon run. Winter is truly our longest season, and summer is short in comparison.

This being true, for the latter part of July and early August, as the weather cooperates, most evenings and on the weekends, the tundra can be flooded with berry seekers. Hondas (local generic term for any ATV) try to maneuver over the *maniqs* (Iñupiaq word for the grassy clumps that grow on the tundra), kids scamper here and there looking for even bigger berries, and scarved heads bob up and down as ladies bend to reach the fruit. Berry season is in full swing. No more waiting. The time is now.

Jesus looked across the valley to the city of Jerusalem, "The field is ripe unto harvest, but the workers are few. Who will go and work in my fields?" (Matt. 9:37). What did He see? Lost souls? A hurting humanity? Bondage? Fear?

I see the people scattered across an area of tundra working steadily to reap a harvest for the winter. How are the workers in the spiritual harvest field working? Am I working? Are you working? Do we see that the time is now? Do we think that tomorrow is more convenient? Jesus needs us to be His workers—workers in the field to labor for a harvest of righteousness.

Just as I am faithful every year to make an effort to pick berries, so I want to be willing to work for an eternal harvest of souls. My dishes sit in the sink, the unfolded laundry lies on the bed, and the floor needs to be mopped. But the berries are ripe. I put aside the earthly things that have no matter in eternity. I make the time to teach Sunday school or whatever the work is that God has given my heart and hands to do. It is now. This is the season.

> As long as it is day, we must do the work of him who sent me. Night is coming when no one can work. (John 9:4)

He Is Here

*E*scape. Running. Provision. Getting out. Over the years, I have had many different motivators for going to the berry patch. When my children were very small, I used to practically run to the tundra. It was an escape. I loved my kids, but it was so refreshing to spend an hour breathing in fresh air and to take a break from hearing any crying. I also loved to pick berries because it fulfilled a sense of purpose in being able to provide for my family. But over the years, an ultimate motivator has moved in to trump all other reasons: time with God.

I breathe in the air, I see the beauty of the colors of the tundra, and I hear the birds and listen to their calling and chattering. I see the cycle of life and feel a part of a whole, big plan. I recognize God in His provision, not just for me, but for all the creatures He has created. And not just the creatures but all living things! I breathe in deep and sense God's presence and feel I am in His sanctuary.

I am in awe at His majesty and the glory of His creation. And I breathe again.

My senses are alive. My heart is stilled. I pray. I worship. I ask. I cry. God is there. His spirit dwells within me. The wind blows across my face, and I pray the Holy Spirit to blow across my life. Blow away the debris, blow in life, blow in love and forgiveness. I'm on my knees picking. I am on my knees repenting. Sweat rolls down the side of my face; tears roll down with them. I breathe again. God is here. God is real. In the isolation of the tundra, in the aloneness of picking, God shows up. I give Him my burdens. He is happy and able to take them from my shoulders and my heart.

What a blessing! What a comfort! Wherever we are is not too far from God. Our God is a big God. My God is a big God. His presence fills the universe. His presence is here and now. I relax. I release. I trust. I acknowledge. I learn.

I am picking again—content in my spirit, content with life because I have spent time in God's sanctuary, in God's garden, and with God's creation. I am a part of all this big world and big plan.

Life is life. It has ups and downs, disappointments and celebrations, pain and healing. Every year has its seasons—the cold and dark of winter, the light of spring, the warmth of summer, and the beauty and bounty of fall time. And God is in it all—the Creator of it all.

I can't pick berries all year round. They aren't available. I must do the work while it is at hand. I must accept the season I am in and do what God has given me to do and find God in that work. It is Him I am working for. This is His world, His church, His family, His creation. He is here.

> Where can I go from your Spirit? Where can I flee from your presence? If I rise on the wings of the dawn, if I settle on the far side of the sea, even there your hand will guide me, your right hand will hold me fast. (Psalm 139:7, 9–10)

Doris winnowing berries on the tundra

About the Author

Doris Van Amburg lives in the rural Iñupiat village of Noatak in northwestern Alaska with her husband of 25 years. There, 70 miles above the Arctic Circle, she has raised her family of four and brings God's Word and Love to those around her. Her family participates in subsistence activities during the arctic seasons including berry picking, using a set net for salmon, ice fishing, hunting for moose and caribou, and gathering wood. As a resident of a fly-in native Alaskan village, she continues in her journey of learning to trust God, His timing, and His provision that comes in all seasons of life.

Printed in the United States
By Bookmasters